to Rambunctious
Ramona
with hoorays!
Margie

The
Stick
Stories

A Collection of Story Dramas
by Margie Brown

Cover Design and Layout: George F. Collopy

Illustrations: Paintings photographed for use as illustrations in this book are located in museums all over the world. Individual credit is given with each picture.

Photography: Doug Gardner
Typography: Virginia Sorich
Mechanical Artist: Stephen Weikart

Library of Congress Catalog Card Number 82-60030
ISBN 0-89390-035-4

Published by Resource Publications, Inc., P. O. Box 444, Saratoga, CA 95071. Printed and bound in the United States of America 4 3

Preface

St. Ignatius of Loyola, in his classic work "The Spiritual Exercises," invites people who are praying in the scriptures to consider the history of the particular mystery, to see a mental representation of the place, to see the biblical characters, to look upon them, to listen to them, to contemplate all they say and do. Then Ignatius invites us to reflect and draw some spiritual fruit from what we have seen and heard.

St. Ignatius invited people to step into the biblical story. To do this people needed to use the gift God gave them in their imaginations. Margie Brown issues a similar invitation to all of us today. Through her stick stories the Word can leap from the page. It can take flesh again in our midst. Blood can flow through old veins and nurture us. Her stories challenge us to meet God the person, to enter into the intimacy of relationship, to walk and talk, to laugh and play, to shake our fists and cry, to live, to die, to wonder and wander together in love. Margie's stories challenge us to reflect on "what we see" and "what we hear" in these stories and our own.

In these simple stories, God's Word does become flesh. We wander with God in the garden. We overhear a wonderfully warm clownversation between God and Eve. We walk a mile with Ruth and Naomi. We marvel at the ways God gets our attention (Moses), our cooperation (Mary), and our love (Jesus).

We are all, large and small, rich and poor, fragmented or whole, stories of God. We all carry God's breath in us. I wish to thank Margie Brown for letting that breath of God in her out. Because of that we have these marvelous stories. The breath and spirit of Margie's stories can quicken the flagging life in each of our own. Listen to them gently and carefully. She holds up for us in her biblical characters a wonderful mirror in which we can each see reflected there the story of God's presence and love in our own lives.

If all you do is read them and enjoy them you will be refreshed. They can do more. Let them invite you to your own dialogues with characters from the Bible and with God. Let them challenge each of you who teach Bible stories to invite your own students to imagine the flesh and blood, the words and deeds of men and women from the Bible just like themselves. Let them lead you to mystery, to faith and to God.

St. Ignatius, in his second introductory observation, says that it is not much knowledge that fills and satisfies the soul, but the intimate understanding and relish of the truth. Anyone who has seen Margie Brown perform her stick stories has been touched and transformed by her intimate understanding and relish of the Good News. So, all you who are hungry, eat. And, all you who are thirsty, drink.

Michael E. Moynahan, SJ

In memory of Wayne Ackerman and Ken Feit, my teachers

Foreword

"The Stick Stories" are a series of biblical animations where a stumbling clown and a simple stick lead us through the characters and conversations of our Judeo-Christian heritage. They are the monologues of my own performances, and grew out of the journey of my clown and my vocation of foolishness.

Over the last decade I have learned clowning in circus and seminary, in sanctuaries and on street corners. I have struggled to find my own style. The clown character which I have developed is how I best share my own story as a vulnerable child of God. As an itinerant performer and teacher, I try also to be a good audience, celebrating others' stories and recognizing the social-political power that can grow from people able to really hear each others' stories.

When I was first asked to write these stories down, I said no. These stories are my prayer, my presentation. How can others pray my prayers? How can hesitant and joyful conversations be translated to the written page? And if others tell these stories, what will I do? People ask me who writes my material, and I laugh. They come so much from my own heart.

But stories are children with a life of their own. Therefore, I took the middle road. I purposely did not write them down as scripts complete with blocking or permission to perform them as I do. But I am glad to share them in a storytelling style and hope that you can find delight in them. My good friend, Tom Woodward, says that there is a difference between "stolen goods" and "derivative material". The difference is that you "use" the former, and in the latter your own creativity is sparked with an "aha!" I hope that these stories can be seeds for your own foolishness and your own stories.

"Therefore, since we are surrounded by so great a cloud of witnesses, let us also lay aside every weight, and sin which clings so closely, and let us run with perserverance the race that is set before us..."

Hebrews 12:1

Contents

Preface 3

Foreword 5

Prelude — The Storyteller 9

Call To Worship 17

Hymn Of Praise 21

Confession 25

Absolution 31

Gloria 35

Teaching 39

Consecration 43

Breaking And Sharing 47

Prayer 49

Commissioning 51

Benediction and Blessing 55

Postlude 59

"Verstellende Vrouw", Vincent Van Gogh, courtesy of Rijksmuseum Kroller-Muller, Holland.

Prelude
The Storyteller

I have met somebody special; a real character, as they say. This person is old and crusty, weatherbeaten and well-lived, full of humorous observations and biting remarks. You see folks like this in subways or on street corners, and it's sometimes hard to tell if they're a man or a woman. This particular person is a storyteller, and an excellent one.

On a front porch somewhere nearby is the stage for those stories spun long into the evening... stories of love and adventure which each person adds to as it goes around the circle. The front porch hangs off of a house that's somewhat tumbled down around the edges. There's a sign in the window, "rooms to rent", because stories don't bring in the money. In back of the house is a beautiful garden tended obviously by someone who knows how to love, and in front of the house sits that same loving person, telling stories to anyone who will listen.

One day I was listening. The longer I listened, the longer I stayed, until I dropped all other plans and joined into the story. For the storyteller knew how to make me feel important, saying to me...

"Let me tell you about storytelling! You need three things. You need a storyteller, and that's me. You need a story that's worth telling, and you need a good storylistener. That's you! Some folks tell them better than others, and some listen better than others, and some stories are more fun to hear than others. But everyone's welcome to sit down and share.

"People today are running around and thinking that they don't have time. It's not just the young folks either. I know that times are hard and everyone has problems, but that's no reason to shut your eyes and ears to the finer things in life like sharing stories.

"La Capeline Rouge — Madam Monet", Claude Oscar Monet (1840-1926), courtesy of the Cleveland Museum of Art, Bequest of Leonard C. Hanna, Jr.

"I know what people think about me. Some folks think I'm mean because I've evicted a lot of folks in my time, and others think I'm crazy because of who I do take in even if they can't pay. Some think I'm old and useless because I like to sit and tell stories. But I think that I tell good stories. They're not the kind that you see on TV that try to sell you something, but they tell about how people are and how people can be.

"I run a respectable house here and I try to treat everyone fairly, but sometimes I have to evict people. It's hard on me, but it's for their own good. The first ones I ever evicted were a young couple named Adam and Eve. I hated to see them go, but they wouldn't follow the rules which I even had posted on the door. I've evicted others, too, but: it's always because of their own doing, like Cain and like Jacob. One time I evicted twelve families at once! Life, like stories, has its own rules, and you have to learn how to listen to them.

"I used to think that if people didn't want to listen, then I must not be a very good storyteller. So I tried to pick up some new ideas and add some jazz to my style. I appeared to Jacob in a dream, and asked some of the neighborhood kids to dance on the fire escape ladder to get his attention. He was afraid to climb the ladder, but we had a good talk anyway. I didn't mean to scare him! That's when I started coming down to the porch to tell my stories.

"I wanted to talk with Moses for a long time, but he kept running away and even left the country for awhile. The neighborhood kids told me about summer camp and telling stories around the campfire. There was a dry bush handy, so I told Moses to take off his shoes and pull up a seat! Like Jacob, he was afraid, too. He took off his shoes but wouldn't sit down. He was shivering with fear; I knew that it wasn't from being cold! Finally we had a good talk, but he had a hard time telling my story to others. I thought about what else I could do to get their attention.

"I remembered the time that I went with two pals to visit Sarah and Abraham. We were having a good laugh because they didn't recognize us. But when they both saw us coming, Sarah made refreshments for us. I thought that that was nice, and a good idea, too!

"Peasants Celebrating Twelfth Night", David Teniers II (1635), courtesy of the National Gallery of Art, Washington, D.C., the Ailsa Mellon Bruce Fund.

"The Strong Man", Honore Daumier, courtesy of the Phillips collection, Washington, D.C.

"So the next time I was with Moses' folks I served refreshments too. I made the manna stuff. It was my own recipe! It was flakier than pie crust, but it spoiled so easily. I learned that people love to sit down and eat, and that's the best time to share stories. I can relax and serve up good plain kosher food.

"I like to feed people... the more the merrier, and simple food is OK. My son Jesus and I used to put out enough bread and fish to feed crowds of folks, and we always had so little to start with! But somehow there were always plenty of leftovers.

"Jesus was a lot like me. He loved food, and he loved stories, and he loved stories about food! He used to tell stories about big banquets and who would or wouldn't be invited, and what folks should wear, and when and where it would be held. I used to swear to myself that he'd been reading those ladies' magazines with the party pictures.

"I had to laugh at Jesus because in the beginning he tried to be fancy, just as I did with the manna. He turned twelve jars of water into wonderful wine! There's a time and a place for being fancy, and Jesus learned also that people thrive best on simple food and simple stories.

"Besides knowing good stories, Jesus knew how to be a good storyteller and a good storylistener. He had a knack for pulling the stories right out of people and helping them feel like the stories they had to tell were important, too. That's what a good storylistener does.

"Sometimes Jesus got into trouble because of the kind of folks that he'd take to lunch. Once he went off and ate with a guy he found in a tree, instead of with the city leaders who had planned a big bash for him. He ate in the fields on the Sabbath which was a no-no and got people even more upset. Jesus just had a good sense of what healthy eating and healthy living were all about. He tried to explain it when he could.

"The last time that he had dinner with his closest friends, it turned out a lot like those banquet stories which he was so fond of telling. They were up there in that upper room, celebrating the Passover with the lamb and all the fixings. They ate themselves full and had seconds on dessert while Jesus told stories.

"But no party is what it looks like in the magazine pictures, and things got complicated, and the party ended on a different note.

"Quarter Meeting",
Anonymous, American ca.
1790, courtesy of the Museum
of Fine Arts, Boston.

"A La Mie", Toulouse Lautrec
(1864-1901), courtest of the .
Museum of Fine Arts, Boston.

"Jesus knew that there would be a problem after the banquet had turned into such a big event. There was all that confusion as everyone tried to get the story straight. They were whispering about Jesus' stories and about his death, and trying to understand how they fit into the picture. The days that followed saw them pricking up their ears and listening hard, but Jesus wanted to give them a nudge to keep on being storytellers, too.

"So he went to eat with them once more. It was very different from the banquet; just a simple fish fry on the beach. There wasn't any soap to clean up from spending the night on the smelly boats, and Jesus had to look all over for the salt. But as the sun was rising, it was a beautiful morning!

"Jesus had told them at the banquet that he loved them. Now he asked if they loved him. Three times he had to ask, because they were just getting used to the idea that they didn't have to be afraid of the answer.

"Yes, they said, Yes. Yes. Then go and do it, he answered them. Feed others, and eat good food yourselves. Tell and hear good stories. Give and receive good things with each other.

"That's what good storysharing is... you need to be a good teller, a good listener, and to have good stories. There are lots of versions of what happened back then with Jesus and his friends: what they ate, what they said, and what it all meant. Groups of people get together even now and tell their version of it and share the food which they think Jesus ate then. They have different kinds of bread and little wafers, wine and grape juice, and sometimes other stuff. But the best part is that each one has his or her own version of the story. We get into good conversations, each one different and each one beautiful. Different folks need different stories, like different food, and I like to work from a big menu.

"I've talked enough and I know that you have other things to do. Next time I see you, though, I'll settle back and it'll be your turn to tell me stories of love and adventure. I know it will be good. Don't be nervous. It just takes practice. I'm looking forward to it."

The clown face reminds us of the universal mask of foolishness which binds all of the ensuing stories together. Each meets God in a unique way, yet the thread of our stumbling simplicity is shared. Likewise, the single stick becomes a walking stick, bush, staff, hobo stick, broom, tree, fishing pole, and cross. The gift continues to be passed on and on in God's continuing creation.

Photos by Doug Gardner, Sacramento, California.

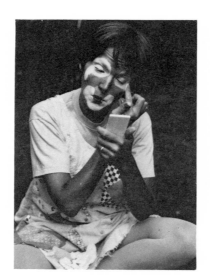 

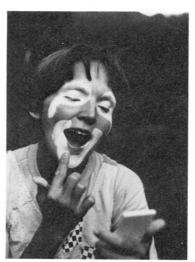 

16

Call To Worship

as God and Eve explore the meaning of
the clown-mask

In the beginning
God created the heavens and the earth
and stars and trees
and skunks and skunk cabbage
and men and women
and then God went away for the weekend.

And when God got back
it was Monday morning
and we all know what Monday morning is like!

So God decided to go and visit Eve
while Adam was at work.
God went in
and sat down at the kitchen table
and said, "hi, Eve!"
and Eve said, "hi, God."

Then God took some make-up
out of her purse and Eve said,
"Hey, God, weren't you a man last week?"
And God said, "Yes, I was,
but this week I wanted to work around the house
so I thought I'd be a woman."
And Eve said, "Oh."

Then God started putting some white stuff
on her face and Eve,
since she was still pretty new
and didn't know any better, said,
"Why are you putting this snow on my face?
I'm going to catch a cold!"
And God said, "Now Eve, pay attention.
Does it feel cold?"
And Eve thought and said, "No."

Then Eve said, "God, am I dead,
and you've come to make me look like a ghost?"
And God laughed, saying,
"Eve! Do you feel like you're dead?"

And God tickled Eve until she laughed and said,
"No!" Then why are you putting this
white stuff on my face?"

"Don't be scared, Eve.
It's a mask, and after awhile
everyone will be wearing masks.
They'll wear masks to pretend
that they're someone else,
or to hide who they really are."

"Why is it white, God?"
"That's because white reflects
every other color.
This is the kind of mask
that people will look in
and see themselves reflected."

With all of this make-up on her face,
Eve started to sneeze
and since Tuesday was dusting day
all of the dust blew up into Eve's face
and God said, "I bless you!"

Then God started putting some red
on Eve's face and she asked,
"Why is it red, God?"

"That's because red is my favorite color!
It's the color of...
Thanksgiving cranberry sauce,
and strawberry jello,
and the planet Mars,
and red light districts,
and apples..."
I thought we decided not to mention
the apples again!"
And God laughed, and continued,
and said, "and blood.
It's a happy, sad, silly, scared,
brave kind of color,
and all of that has to be shown, too."

Then God took a pencil
and started putting some lines on Eve's face
and she said, "God, don't do that!
You'll make me look old,
and then Adam won't love me anymore."
God said, "that's not true.
And besides, I have to put the lines on."

"Are you going to put lines around everything?"
"No, some places will have lines around them
and other places it will just blend together."
Eve asked, "How do you know the difference?"
"If you live long enough,
and pay attention, and listen carefully,
you just get to know
where the lines have to be drawn
and where things can blend."

"God, are you sure
that everyone will be wearing a mask like this?"
"Now Eve, you weren't listening!
I said that everyone would be wearing masks.
But this is a special kind of mask
to remind the other people
that they're wearing masks."

"So why do I have to be the first one?"
"I didn't choose that for you, Eve.
I'm just trying to help you out.
Because you're the first person in history
who's going to be misunderstood."

And Eve didn't say anything
because God had gotten up to go
and when the door opened
there was a blizzard outside which blew in
and covered her face
and when Eve could see again
God was gone.

*"Cliff Dwellers", George
Wesley Bellows (1913),
courtesy of the Los Angeles
Museum of Art, purchased with
county funds.*

Hymn of Praise

as God and all creation gather in the
Garden of Eden

Good morning, garden!
It's me, God!
I brought the news for you this morning.
Wake up, everyone!

I have to tell you that the news isn't very good...
I have to go away.
But I'll be back as soon as I can!
You know that Adam and Eve left yesterday
and I'm going to follow along behind them
because they'll be needing some help.

Don't look so sad!
My dear Oak Tree, cheer up!
You're strong and deep-rooted
and I'm depending on you
to help out while I'm gone.
A going-away present?
Thank you, Oak Tree!
An acorn cup!
It'll make a good drinking cup.
I'm sure that I'll get thirsty;
it'll be a long journey.

And my beautiful Roses!
Don't be sad; I'll be back as soon as I can.
You're strong, too, in a different kind of way.
I want you to watch over all of the flowers.
A present for me, too?
A thorn!
And a nice sharp one, too.
It'll make a good needle;
I might need to make some repairs along the way.

"Girls Throwing Flowers", *Karl*
Hofer (1934), courtesy of the
Art Institute of Chicago.

And you, my chattering Squirrel!
Run along and tell the animals who couldn't be here
that I'll be back as soon as I can
and I'll be listening for your chatter
to hear if I'm getting close when I return.
Nuts! They'll make a good lunch.
Thank you, Squirrel.

Dove! Dove! Come here please.
I'd like to have a traveling companion.
Would you come with me?
Hurry and go pack.
And, Dove! Only one suitcase!

My beautiful Tree of Knowledge!
Don't look so guilty!
It wasn't your fault.
They knew what their choices were.
I need you to keep the morale up.
I still love you.
What's this? A good strong branch.
One of your best.
It'll make a good walking stick.
Thank you.

Dove!
Are you ready?
One more kiss, then.

Goodbye, everybody!
Be good to each other!
I'll be back as soon as I can.
Goodbye!

*"Allegory of Summer and
Winter",* Giovanni Battista
Pittoni (1687-1767), courtesy of
the Dayton Art Institute,
museum purchase with funds
provided by the Institute Ball
1965, and the Virginia V.
Blakeney Endowment.

Confession

as Moses makes excuses at the burning
bush

C-c-come on, s-s-sheep.
Over this way.
N-no, get back!
There's a fire!

FIRE!
Somebody call the fire department!
Call Smokey the Bear!
There's a talking bush on fi...
a talking bush?
On fire?

Hey!
Are you talking to me?
Who's in there?
How did you get in there?
What's your name?

"I am"?

"I am" who?

"I am who I am".
Sounds like an Abbott and Costello routine.

Do you have a nickname?
GOD?
God, is that you?
What are you doing in there?
How did you get in there?
I thought it was the other place
that was supposed to be hot?

No thanks.
I don't need a job.
I'm taking care of my sheep.

What?
The Pharoah.
Let the people go.

"Show in New York", *Robert Henri (1865-1929), courtesy of National Gallery of Art, Washington, D.C.*

God, do you know what that will sound like?
Listen to this...

"Hey, Pharoah, let the people go!"
"Says who?"
"I am!"

That's not fair, God!

How will you help me?
Pick up the stick?
God, put the fire out first, please!

Now what?
Throw it down!
God, make up your mind.

Aaaugh!
God, you know I hate snakes!
Turn it back!
Stay...
stay...
OK, I've got it now.

Pretty good trick, God.
But what if it doesn't fool Pharoah?
Plan B.

What's plan B?
To the river...
touch the water...
Blood! You can't do that!
The Pharoah can drink that Perrier stuff
but the people have to drink the water...
What if it doesn't work?
Plan C.
How many plans do you have, God?
As many as you need.

So say that we try all of your plans
and the Pharoah lets the people go.
Then what?
They can't all fit in my apartment.

Over there.
God, there's a whole lot of water in the way.
The stick again.
What am I going to do,
wrap a towel around the stick
and dry a path?

Trust you?

Trust you!

I don't know...

The whole thing is so crazy,
it just might work!

"The Tramway", *Mary Cassatt*, *20th century*, *courtesy of the National Gallery of Art*, *Washington*, *D.C.*, *Rosenwald Collection.*

Absolution

as Ruth and Naomi share a song of love
and forgiving faith

Mom!
Come on, Mom!
Come on Naomi, keep up!

You look so tired.
Here, I'll carry your bag for awhile.
Why don't you sit here on the curb.
Just keep your thumb out.
OK, you can stick your foot out.

We're going to make it, Naomi.
We've got to get to Bethlehem by nightfall.
Are there any sandwiches left?
I wonder how that other hitch-hiker is doing
who we saw this morning.
You know, that one with the dove?
Haven't seen them in a while.

They won't pick us up if we're crying!
Please don't cry. You'll get their upholstery wet.
We have to keep our spirits up
and it won't seem so far.
I'll sing a song for us,
but keep your thumb out, OK?

Here's Ruth and old Naomi,
   going down the road...
No man or God to help them out
   by carrying their load. (Cha-cha-cha!)

My mom tried to get rid of me
   and said I had to go...
but I made a funny face at her
   and kissed her and said "no". (Remember?)

Your God will be my God,
   and your home will be my home...
we'll share the same apartment
   and together we will roam!

*"Man with Sack", Malewitch
(1911), courtesy of the Stedelijk
Museum, Amsterdam.*

Your bathroom will be my bathroom;
    I'll let you use my towel...
I'll sing you jokes and tell you...whoops;
I'll tell you jokes and sing you songs,
I'll buy you a new cow.

Your man has died...my man has died...
    I wished I could die too.
But now I'm feeling stronger
    and I'll take good care of you.

You said you have a God above...
    you used to tell me so.
So come on, God, stick out your thumb,
    and the three of us will go!

So goodbye to Moab, it's Bethlehem or bust...
we're not going to sit around and let us go to rust!

Hey,
that eighteen wheeler is stopping!
Ten-four, good buddy!
Here we come!

"A Suffolk Child", John
Constable *(1835), courtesy of
the Victoria and Albert
Museum, London.*

Gloria

as Mary responds to the angel's message

Coming. I'm coming!

Good morning.
Yes, I'm Mary.
How do you do Gabriel.
Can I help you?
A message.

The Lord is with me.
I don't see anybody...
do you have someone out in the hall?

I've found favor with the Lord.
You go tell him that I like him, too
but if you'll excuse me I have a lot of work to do.

No, I don't understand!
Blessed be the fruit of my broom?
Mister, I have all the sweeping up that I need.

Blessed be the fruit of my womb?
You're not making any sense!
If you have a message for me,
just say it straight and simple.

Oh.
That's pretty straight and simple.

You're telling me
that I'm going to have a baby.
Mister, I don't think
that you can do that kind of thing door to door.

You're serious, aren't you?
That's a pretty crazy proposition.
Why would I want to do that?
I'm not even married.

Vincent Van Gogh, "Zadier",
courtesy of Stedelijk Museum,
Amsterdam.

This must be some special kind of kid
to come this way.
Well, what kind?
Yes,...
yes...
really?...
Jesus Christ...
MAGNIFICENT!

Well mister,
if what you're saying is true,
then what can I say?
I guess you can go tell your boss
that he's got himself a little mother.

Am I scared?
No...
Yes...
It is scary, and people will talk,
but how can I pass up an adventure like this?

Yes.
Good bye.
Thank you...
I think.
Have a nice day!

Joe?
Hey, Joe!
Guess what?
No,
you'll never guess!

"Jittoku Laughing at the Moon", *School of Geimi, 15th century, courtest of the Museum of Fine Arts, Boston.*

Teaching

as Zaccheus discovers the heart of Jesus'
ministry

Zac! Come over here Zaccheus!
Don't you want to see the parade?

        No! I hate parades!
        I'm too short!

Oh Zac, you're such a sourpuss.
You're always complaining.
We'll get up close to the curb,
then you will be able to see.

        No! I hate parades!
        I'm too short!
        All the dogs think I'm a fire hydrant!

Zac, you think you're the only
one with problems. We can find
a way...you can climb that fire
escape, or stand on that car, or
climb that tree, or something!

        Look! Just because I'm short
        doesn't mean I'm a little kid.
        I haven't climbed a tree
        in thirty years!

Then it's about time you did.
Come on, I'll help you up.

        Oh, all right. Here I go.

What do you see, Zac?

        Just hold on!
        I see them coming!
        There's a big crowd of people,
        twelve or thirteen of them,
        and there's a guy in front; he's real tall!

What else do you see, Zac?

"Samuel and Eli", *William
Drost, 17th century, courtesy of
the Art Institute of Chicago.*

Just hold on!
They're coming down the street,
in front of the bank,
through the gas station,
up to the light,
and they stopped for something...

What's the matter?
Did a kid run into the
street or something?

Just hold on!
I'm looking!
I can't really tell,
but it seems like
they're looking over there...

Don't go away!
Stay up there!
I'll try to find out.
Hey, mister!
What's going on?
Yeah?
I'd better tell him!
Oh, Za-ac!
You'd better come on down!
That guy over there, Jesus,
says that he wants to
have lunch with you today!
Ha, ha!

With me?
Oh oh.
Tell him...
that I'm not hungry!
Oh...
watch out.
I'm coming down.

Hello?
Are you Mister Jesus?
How do you do, Mister Jesus?
You want to have lunch
with me today?
Wow!
I feel five feet tall!

"The Dancing Couple", Jan Steen (1626-1679), courtesy of the National Galleryof Art, Washington, D.C., Widener Collection.

Consecration

as a stranger stumbles into it

Hello.
May I come in?
I'm awfully hungry,
and no other place seems to be open.
I saw all of the people here
and thought there was no harm in asking.

Thank you.
This looks like a good crowd.
Twelve.
Good number for bridge, eh?

Yes.
A beautiful table.
Looks handcarved.
A good piece of wood.

What is he doing?
The man with the dishpan and the paper towels.
Washing their feet?
Look, that one wants a shampoo, too!
What kind of party is this?

Here comes the food!
Bread?
Good. Pumpernickel.
He's taking off the twisty-tie,...
What did he say?
Eat up?
"This is my body."
I don't understand.

At last, here comes the wine!
Paper cups. I'll take one.
Cheers!
What does he mean,
"This is my blood"?

"The Kitchenmaid", Johannes Vermeer (1632-1675), courtesy of the Rijksmuseum, Amsterdam.

He's going away?
He said that?
I told you this was a strange party.
If he likes it, then where is he going?
No, not clear at all.
Is he coming back?
Some say yes.
Some say no.
And you?

Confusing.

*"Female Figure with Flying Drapery and Raised Arms",
Pelligrino Tiboldi (1527-1596),
courtesy of the Los Angeles
Museum of Art.*

Breaking and Sharing

as Jesus moves from the garden to the cross

Dad?
Hey, Dad,
I'm here in the garden of Gethsemene.
Can we have a talk?

How come all of the other kids get the keys to the car,
and I get the keys to the kingdom?

How come I can't just be a winemaker
like mom wanted me to be?

How come you brought me up to be myself,
but the older I get,
the more I look like you?

It's not fair, Dad!
I'm not the kind of kid that you think I am.
I get really nervous when I heal the sick,
and I contradict myself a lot,
and my friends don't know who I am.
I don't even know, sometimes.

Can't we just call it off?

OK...

OK!

OK, I'll do it.

You heard me.
I'll do it.

Dad?
You still love me, Dad?

Blow me a kiss?

"Crouching Tahitian Girl",
Paul Gauguin (1848-1903),
courtesy of the Art Institute of
Chicago.

Prayer

as Mary Magdalene struggles with her
own cross

Jesus!
Jesus, it's me, Mary Magdalene!
I'm still here.
All the others have gone,
but I'm still here.

Jesus,
I don't know what to do!
I don't know what to say.

What?
Are you thirsty?
Can I get you a coke or something?
I don't know what...

Jesus,
don't die!
Please don't die.
If you die, then I want to die too.
If you die, then I want to...

Ouch!
A splinter...

"The Wateran", Winslow Homer (1898), courtesy of the Art Institute of Chicago.

Commissioning

as Peter begins again with breakfast on
the beach

Nobody likes me, everybody hates me,
guess I'll go eat worms...
Bite off their heads and suck out their guts,
guess I'll go eat worms...

Hey, you stupid fish!
This is the great Peter!
Haven't you heard of me?
I'm not standing here for my health!
I'm cold and tired and lonely
and my friends are mad at me,
and you won't bite the stupid worm!

Here fish, fishy...

Good morning!
What? No, nothing!
Maybe a cold!
On the other side of the boat?
What do you know about it?
OK, OK...

Hey mister!
You were right!
Thanks a lot!

Hey, mister...
Haven't I seen you somewhere...
Jesus?
Is that you, Lord?
Wait right there, I'm coming over!

Uh,
Je-sus,
could you do me one little favor?
I don't want to get my clothes wet.
Oh come on, Jesus, you did it before!
Just a little walk on the water...
how about just up to the knees?
Alright! I'm coming.

"Woman with Loaves", Pablo Picasso (1906), courtesy of the Philadelphia Museum of Art, given by Charles E. Ingersoll.

Jesus!
It's really you!
You have a fire going and everything.
Here's a fish for it.
Jesus, what's going on?

Do I love you?

Of course I love you!
Didn't I just jump into the water with all my clothes on for you?

Then feed your sheep?
Jesus, you've got sheep now?
We all thought you were dead,
and you were off starting a new business?
I don't understand...

Do I love you?

Jesus, you know that I do.
I mean, like one of the guys,...
but you know that I love you.

Then feed your lambs.
Jesus, I can't feed lambs.
I'm a fisherman.
All I have are fish and worms.
Lambs don't eat worms.

Do I love you?
I think I do.
I try to.

That's what I thought you'd say.
Feed your sheep.

Jesus, I hate to tell you this,
but I don't see any sheep.
I don't know what you're talking about.
I don't see a sheep...
there's not a lamb...
there's not a ram...
there's not a ewe...

you?
Feed them?
Feed the people?

But Jesus, there are too many of them!
It's so much work...

Jesus?
Jesus?
Where did you go?

Anybody want a worm?

"Le Savoyard", Antoine Watteau (1684-1721), courtesy of the Art Institute of Chicago.

Benediction and Blessing

as the story continues throughout the world

Howdy.
Sure, you can sit here.
Yes. Hot.
Going far?
I'm not sure either.
Just to the end of the road maybe.
Who knows.

Yes, I found it a while back.
It's a good strong one; I like it.
I've been whittling these designs in it.
Hard to tell what they are, but I know.
I guess that's what's important.

All kinds of uses.
It helps me get up hills.
I'm not growing any younger.
Holds up my tarp when it rains.
Hang my bandana on it when I have to stake my claim.
This here's my territory!
Play fetch with my dog.
Scratch my back.
Look for lost coins in the curb.
Protect myself, if I have to.
If I was in one place long enough,
maybe I'd raise tomatoes on it!

Yeah, yours looks the same.
Like a well-worn friend.
You can always tell the travelers
by their sticks.
Nothing fancy or fashionable.
Just enough for what you need.

This is all the food I've got today,
but I'll be glad to share it.
And that sweater's falling right off you.
Here's an extra one that I found at my last camp.
It's starting to turn cold again.

"Head of Christ", *Rembrandt*,
from the Staatliche Museum,
Berlin.

It's nice sharing stories with you,
taking it easy.
Your hands look like that old stick;
gnarled up, full of surprises.
Strong and gentle.
Trade?
Now that would be something.
It's OK. Sure.
This here's a nice stick.
See where it takes me.
See where mine takes you.
That's nice.
You going far?
Yeah, a little while together.
We'll see what happens.
I'd like that, too.

"Street at Dusk", *Lyonel*
Feininger (1871-1956), courtesy
of Kunstmuseum Hannover mit
Smmlung Sprengel, copyright
Cosmo Press, Geneva.

Postlude

Howdy, everybody! It's me, Angela, and I'm glad to see you all. Are you going up to the party at my friend Grace's house? You know that house way up on the hill, the one that looks almost like a castle. It isn't full of fancy stuff, but it's so big and roomy and always full of people. And my friend Grace is so queenly, too, and everyone loves her so.

I went to a party there last year, and the place was crowded with all kinds of people. I may not remember you if you were there because of everything else that happened that night.

I'd just arrived when Grace called me aside into the living room, saying that she wanted to have a talk.

"Why Grace, what's the matter? You look like you've got something on your mind."

"I just want to talk with you for a minute, Angel," she said. She always called me Angel. "About being my friend. We are good friends?"

"Why, of course we are. We have been for years. What are you talking like that for?"

"I know that we are, but I've been watching you lately and I just have to tell you what's been bothering me."

I got a scary feeling in my throat and said, "What's wrong, Grace? Tell me."

She blushed a little and said, "Angel, I don't hardly know how to say this, but I want to talk with you about eating. About if you'd give me something to eat if I needed it."

"Grace, I'm surprised at you! We've eaten together plenty of times, and you know I'd be there if you were the least bit hungry."

"I know that's true, Angel, but some of the neighborhood kids told me that you wouldn't let them in the church supper last week because they didn't have food to bring."

"Tahitian Woman with Children", Paul Guaguin (1901), courtesy of the Art Institute of Chicago.

"But they're just a bunch of kids. It's not fair if they don't contribute."

"What kind of hunger is that, where you have to have food before you can get it? You know that money is tight in that area, and it seems like you have a different idea than they do about what's fair."

I started making excuses but she stopped me and said, "and Angel, if I was thirsty, would you have a drink for me?"

"Grace, you're being silly. You know we're always having coffee or tea together.

"I know that, and you know too that water's been scarce this season and they tell us on the radio to be careful, but you've been watering and washing out in your yard a lot. Not that I'm spying on you, but it just gives me an uncomfortable feeling to see you with a guzzling attitude. I don't know if you would hear when I tell you that I'm thirsty for something."

I was embarrassed now but she started right up again. "And if I was naked, would you give me something to wear?"

I laughed out loud at that one. "Now Grace, you know that you're not the kind to go running naked down the street, and nobody in this town is so poor that they have no clothes on. There are places to go to get clothes for free or cheap."

"But Angel, the way that you look at people who aren't dressed as you choose, they might as well be naked. You don't clothe them with dignity or respect. And what about a place to stay?"

I was angry now and wanted to scream at her. "You know you've stayed at my place plenty of times. What are you talking about?"

"Remember the town meeting and the refugee discussion? You said that our town couldn't handle it and they should go somewhere ese. Well, our something is better than their nothing, but you didn't even want to discuss it."

"...and if I was sick," she went right on, "would you take care of me the way I needed taking care of?"

"Grace, you know I've got a houseful of kids who are always getting sick, and I help out all kinds of folks and shut-ins. You're just plain telling lies about me now."

"I know that you're good about the kind of sick that chicken soup can cure. But there are scarier kinds of sick, and you shy away as if those people didn't exist. If something goes wrong with me that kind of way, I'm scared that you'd be far away. It's kind of like if I was in prison, I know that you wouldn't visit me."

I jumped now. "You're not being fair at all! You're accusing me of all of the world's problems, and now you want me all lovey-dovey with the criminals, those who really hurt people and deserve to be locked up. What kind of person do you think I can be?"

"I'm not trying to be unfair, honey. I know that you do the best that you can. Prisoners are hard to understand, but they're still people, Angel. If we forget that, then we're in trouble, because everyone has their own kind of prison. Angel, you know that my son was working over there in that troubled country."

"I know that, Grace."

"And you know that they've been having trouble with the government putting all the religious folks in jail."

"Yes, I read about it just a little in the papers."

"Well, they threw my son in prison, too, and it was in the papers here, and nobody asked. Nobody asked at all. And I felt like I was in prison too."

"Oh, Grace, I'm so sorry. How is he?"

"He's dead now. They killed my boy, Jesus, and the news was all around, but nobody paid it no mind."

Now I knew what she was trying to say. I felt terrible, like I was homeless and sick and thirsty and all, too. And I didn't know how to get out of it.

But Grace and I are good friends, and we talked and cried about it until I could laugh. I feel kind of sheepish when I look back at everything. I'll be going up to the house again tonight, a different person yet the same all at once. There'll be all kinds of folks there. Maybe I'll see you there. It's that kind of party.